D0602483

THE GREAT BARRIER REEF

by Rebecca Kraft Rector

FOCUS READERS

FOCUS READERS

WWW.FOCUSREADERS.COM

Focus Readers is distributed by North Star Editions:
sales@northstareditions.com | 888-417-0195

Produced for Focus Readers by Red Line Editorial.

Content Consultant: Jodi Schwarz, PhD, Associate Professor of Biology, Vassar College

Photographs ©: vlad61/iStockphoto, cover, 1; JoshuaWells_Photography/iStockphoto, 4–5; KJA/iStockphoto, 6; Red Line Editorial, 9, 21; asmithers/iStockphoto, 10–11; Krofoto/ Shutterstock Images, 13; Tomas Sykora/Shutterstock Images, 15; Dkart/iStockphoto, 16–17; Searsle/iStockphoto, 18; Global_Pics/iStockphoto, 23; Pete Niesen/Shutterstock Images, 24–25; chameleonseye/iStockphoto, 27; Darkydoors/Shutterstock Images, 28

ISBN
978-1-63517-514-1 (hardcover)
978-1-63517-586-8 (paperback)
978-1-63517-730-5 (ebook pdf)
978-1-63517-658-2 (hosted ebook)

Library of Congress Control Number: 2017948110

Printed in the United States of America
Mankato, MN
November, 2017

ABOUT THE AUTHOR

Rebecca Kraft Rector is a writer, librarian, and researcher. She is the author of novels, nonfiction books, and more than 100 nonfiction articles.

TABLE OF CONTENTS

CHAPTER 1

ALIVE AND COLORFUL

An orange-and-white clownfish swims through warm waters. It passes sea cucumbers and giant clams. Colorful corals create a garden of pink flowers and green trees. A blue sea star lies atop the coral. Anemones wave gently in the warm ocean water. Life in the Great Barrier **Reef** is active and beautiful.

The Great Barrier Reef is full of life.

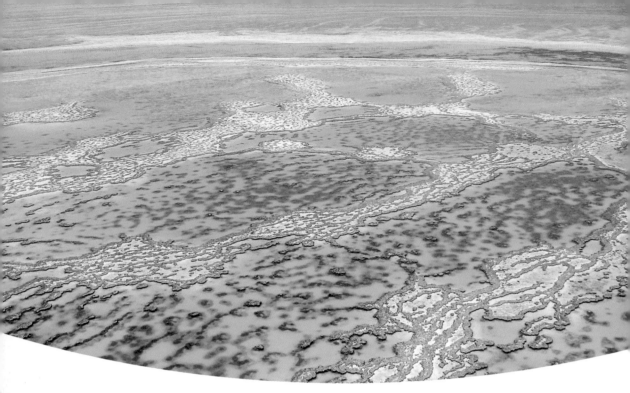

The Great Barrier Reef is known for its bright blue water.

The Great Barrier Reef is in the Coral Sea, off Australia's northeastern coast. It is Earth's largest coral reef system. Coral reefs are ridges of limestone found just below the water. The limestone is made from skeletons of dead corals. Living corals grow on the surface of the ridge.

The Great Barrier Reef is the world's largest living structure. The reef is approximately 1,430 miles (2,300 km) long. It is nearly 135,000 square miles (350,000 sq km) in area. That is roughly the size of Italy. Astronauts can even see the reef from space.

TRADITIONAL OWNERS

Two native groups have long-lasting ties to the Great Barrier Reef. These are the Aboriginal and Torres Strait Islander peoples. The reef plays a strong part in their traditional lives. It influences their **culture**. Their stories, art, and music are connected to the Great Barrier Reef.

The Great Barrier Reef is made up of approximately 3,000 coral reefs. There are also hundreds of islands and **cays**. Close to the Australian shore, the water around the reef is shallow. Farther out, it is more than 1.2 miles (1.9 km) deep.

These differences mean there are **habitats** for an enormous variety of life. Sea life ranges from tiny **algae** to large whales. Creatures such as birds and reptiles live there, too.

The water is warm throughout the year. It stays 70 to 100 degrees Fahrenheit (21 to 38°C) at the surface. The water is also very clear in most places. This makes scuba diving a popular tourist experience.

MAP OF THE GREAT BARRIER REEF

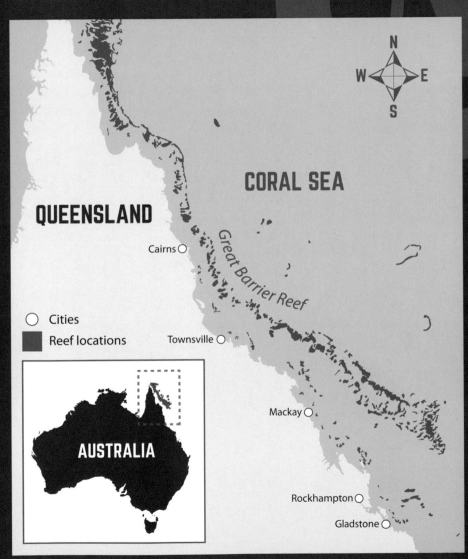

N
W E
S

CORAL SEA

QUEENSLAND

Cairns ○

Great Barrier Reef

○ Cities
■ Reef locations

Townsville ○

AUSTRALIA

Mackay ○

Rockhampton ○

Gladstone ○

CHAPTER 2

FORMING THE GREAT BARRIER REEF

Approximately 25 million years ago, sea levels were high. At this time, reefs began forming along the northeastern coast of Australia. The reefs were made of coral.

Corals are animals with a body shape called a polyp. Coral polyps can bud new polyps. In this way, a coral colony is built.

Changing water levels over millions of years helped form the Great Barrier Reef.

A colony is made of thousands of polyps that all came from one original polyp.

As thousands of years passed, the old corals died. New corals grew on top of them. Eventually, the corals formed reefs. This was the beginning of the Great Barrier Reef.

WORKING TOGETHER

Corals grow in tropical water. This water is low in nutrients, meaning very little life can grow there. But corals do. That's because their cells provide homes for tiny algae. Meanwhile, these algae provide food for the corals. This type of relationship is called symbiosis. The corals then serve as a food source, which allows other **species** to live in these tropical waters.

Coral polyps have soft bodies, similar to jellyfish.

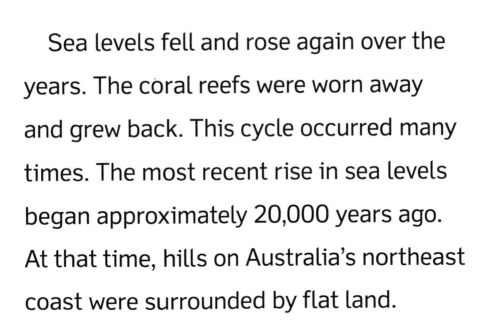

Sea levels fell and rose again over the years. The coral reefs were worn away and grew back. This cycle occurred many times. The most recent rise in sea levels began approximately 20,000 years ago. At that time, hills on Australia's northeast coast were surrounded by flat land.

The flat land was a continental shelf. Sea levels rose, and the continental shelf flooded. The hills became islands surrounded by water.

Approximately 10,000 years ago, the Great Barrier Reef began to form again. Corals grew around the islands and created reefs. The reefs were still close to land. So these are called fringing reefs.

The sea levels continued to rise and covered the smaller islands. Coral reefs then grew over them. The taller islands were not covered by water. These islands are called continental islands. New fringing reefs grew near them. In this way, the Great Barrier Reef was formed.

Reefs formed around ancient landforms to create the Great Barrier Reef.

CHAPTER 3

PLANTS AND ANIMALS

The Great Barrier Reef provides habitats for numerous life-forms. Animals live in the water, on the islands, and on the coral cays. Living among the animals are algae, seaweeds, and plankton. Each contributes to the reef **ecosystem**.

The life-forms living in the Great Barrier Reef rely on one another for survival.

A sea turtle swims near the ocean floor at the Great Barrier Reef.

The microscopic algae living inside corals feed the corals and help them grow. This means that corals can create their limestone skeletons. When they join with the skeletons of other corals, they create the hard rock of the reef.

Approximately 500 species of seaweed grow in the Great Barrier Reef. Certain kinds of tiny plants and animals make up a group called plankton. Algae is a kind of plankton. Plankton is an important source of food for corals and other animals.

More than 2,600 plant species grow on the islands and coral cays. Mangrove trees and seagrasses grow along the coast.

MANGROVES

Mangroves are trees that grow along the shore. Their bare roots can be seen above the mud or water. Mangroves protect the shore from wind and waves. They also filter **sediment**. This keeps the sediment from smothering corals. Mangroves provide habitats above the water and below. It is possible for corals to grow in their shade.

Seagrass meadows provide hiding places for small fish. Seagrass is also a source of food for some water animals. Green Island is a coral cay. It is home to a rainforest.

Thousands of animal species live in the water. More than 450 species of hard corals make up the reefs. At least 150 species of soft coral live there as well. Soft corals do not have hard skeletons. They do not build reefs. They sometimes look like small plants or trees.

Many animals also live on the islands and coral cays. More than 200 species of seabirds and shorebirds are found there.

In addition, several mammal species live near the Great Barrier Reef. It is home to a rare species of wallaby. Other island mammals include fruit bats, koalas, and water rats.

REEF ECOSYSTEM

Various species live in different parts of the Great Barrier Reef.

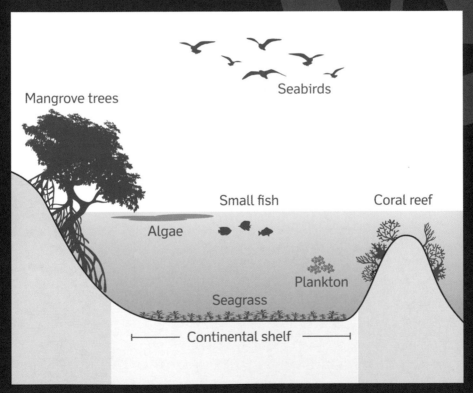

Seabirds

Mangrove trees

Small fish

Coral reef

Algae

Plankton

Seagrass

Continental shelf

CLOWNFISH AND SEA ANEMONES

Sea anemones look like underwater flowers. However, they are actually animals that eat fish. Anemones are similar to corals, but they do not have skeletons. They attach to a rock or to the seabed. From this position, the anemones use their poisonous **tentacles** to sting fish.

The clownfish is not like other fish. It is safe from the anemone's poison. The clownfish has a mucus coating. This protects it from the sea anemone. Because of this, the clownfish can live among the sea anemone tentacles. It is safe from its enemies there. It eats bits of fish that the anemone leaves. In this way, the anemone helps the clownfish.

The clownfish helps the anemone, too. The clownfish sometimes defends the anemone from

Clownfish and sea anemones work together for survival.

butterfly fish, which eat anemones. At times, the clownfish also lures other fish to the anemone so it can eat.

CHAPTER 4

THE GREAT BARRIER REEF TODAY

The Great Barrier Reef is one of the Seven Natural Wonders of the World. It is a natural wonder because of its size and beauty. It is also a UNESCO World Heritage Site. This means it has value to the entire world.

The Great Barrier Reef is an important resource. Many fish species live there.

The Great Barrier Reef supports many kinds of life.

They support fisheries. The reef also protects the land from strong waves and rising waters during storms. In addition, sources for new medicines have been found in coral reef algae and animals.

Approximately two million people visit the Great Barrier Reef every year. Some sail around the islands or view the reef from an airplane. Scuba diving is also popular. Objects 100 feet (30 m) underwater can be seen easily. Guidelines protect both people and the reefs.

Climate change is a major threat to the Great Barrier Reef. The temperature of the sea is rising. This has led to new coral diseases. When the temperature gets too

Divers must be careful not to damage the corals by touching them.

high, corals also lose the algae that live inside them. The corals then turn white, in a process known as coral bleaching. If the temperature stays too high, the corals can die.

Coral bleaching could kill the Great Barrier Reef.

Bleaching is the greatest threat to coral reefs. In 2017, scientists announced that large portions of the Great Barrier Reef were dead. High water temperatures were to blame.

The reef faces other threats, too. Runoff from farms and other local developments pollutes the corals. Overfishing can be a problem. Divers and boats can damage the corals as well.

Governments and other groups are trying to protect the Great Barrier Reef. The Great Barrier Reef Marine Park was formed in 1975. Park officials manage the area and regulate private development.

The Great Barrier Reef is a place of amazing beauty and variety. It is home to a large number of plants and animals. However, the future of the Great Barrier Reef is uncertain. Saving it will require many people working together.

FOCUS ON
THE GREAT
BARRIER REEF

Write your answers on a separate piece of paper.

1. Write a sentence describing the main ideas of Chapter 4.

2. Would you like to swim in the Great Barrier Reef? Why or why not?

3. What is the main cause of coral bleaching?
- **A.** runoff from farms
- **B.** careless scuba divers
- **C.** rising water temperatures

4. What might happen if algae did not grow over coral skeletons and join them together?
- **A.** The reef might float away.
- **B.** The reef might have no food.
- **C.** The reef might grow stronger.

Answer key on page 32.

GLOSSARY

algae
Plant-like organisms that produce oxygen and live within corals or in the water.

cays
Small islands of coral or sand.

culture
The way a group of people live; their customs, beliefs, and laws.

ecosystem
The collection of living things in a natural area.

habitats
The types of places where plants or animals normally grow or live.

reef
A ridge of sharp rock, coral, or sand just below the ocean surface.

sediment
Material that settles to the bottom of the water.

species
A group of animals or plants that are similar.

tentacles
Long, flexible arms around an animal's head or mouth.

TO LEARN MORE

BOOKS

Medina, Nico. *Where Is the Great Barrier Reef?* New York: Grosset & Dunlap, 2016.

Murphy, Julie. *Coral Reefs Matter.* Minneapolis: Abdo Publishing, 2016.

Woolf, Alex. *Sailing the Great Barrier Reef.* New York: Gareth Stevens, 2015.

NOTE TO EDUCATORS

Visit **www.focusreaders.com** to find lesson plans, activities, links, and other resources related to this title.

INDEX

Answer Key: **1.** Answers will vary; **2.** Answers will vary; **3.** C; **4.** B